I WROTE THIS INSTEAD OF SLEEPING

a memoir in fragments by Shelby Rose

Cover design: [Shelby Rose]
Interior design: [Shelby Rose]
First Edition
Printed in the United States of America

ISBN: 979-8-2956-1564-1

ACKNOWLEDGEMENTS

To my friends and family who listened to me cry, rant,
spiral, overthink, and still showed up the next day
I love you more than all the sleep I lost writing this.

Thank you for keeping me alive, hydrated, and only
slightly less dramatic than I wanted to be.

For the ones who stayed.
For the ones who loved me through it.
For the ones who wouldn't let me lose myself
completely.

Thank you.

A NOTE FROM THE AUTHOR

written by present-day shelby rose

I didn't know then what I know now.
When I wrote these pages, I wasn't trying to make a
book. I wasn't trying to be poetic or profound. I was
just trying to survive myself—minute by minute, hour
by hour—during one of the ugliest heartbreaks I've ever
lived through. I couldn't see beyond the day in front of
me. I couldn't imagine that I would ever be whole
again.

But reading this now, years later, I see something
different. I see a girl who broke open instead of
breaking apart. I see honesty, even when it was messy.
I see poetry, even when I didn't know I was writing any.
I see the first version of the woman I've finally become.
This book is a time capsule. A portrait of heartbreak,
yes, but also a map out of it. It's not perfect—neither
was I. Neither is life.
That's the beauty of it.

If you're reading this, I hope you see parts of yourself in
these pages. And more than that, I hope you see your
way through.

— *shelby rose*

I

THE SHATTERING

MARCH 1ST 2020

12:19 AM

i found a roll of toilet paper in my bed. it's been there
since last night.
the worst part is that your phone isn't going off
anymore, because he was the only one you texted all
the time. now you have no one to talk to.
you're just as alone as you thought you were.
did you really think you deserved somebody normal?
you stupid idiot.

DREAD

are you ever afraid to go to bed? not to sleep, i mean.
but to get in bed, turn off the lights, shut down your tv
or laptop, and close your eyes—only to be trapped with
all the lonely thoughts you're terrified to face.
or feeling pathetic enough to open your laptop and pull
up the fucking text edit application on your ten-year-
old mac and type out your inner monologue in a font
that looks like an old school typewriter.
but seriously.
i am afraid to go to sleep.

DULLNESS

do you want to hear something else comical? the fact
that everything feels dull. i'm not even poetic, but
actually—
music sucks. my vision is blurry half the time. eating?
yeah, right. everything tastes like nothing.
it's honestly pathetic how much this has affected me.
i'm embarrassed to even write it. maybe if i don't talk
about it or admit it, then it's not real.
nothing feels like reality.
not even 24 hours in and i feel catatonic.
i stared at the corner of my wall for about 30 minutes
this morning. i'm watching myself from the outside,
like i'm not even in my own body.
how is this actually happening...

WORK

it's just fucking embarrassing having to go to work and
have people feel bad for you. then having to talk to a
customer about their fucking "peppery pasta" that's
supposedly inedible.
sir. in the grand scheme of the world, your pasta
doesn't mean shit.
have a nice day, thank you for coming.
i have to get up at seven in the morning.
bye.

FOUR DAYS LATER

update: i still feel dead inside, and this isn't a
temporary breakup. i've realized it's actually
happening, and i'm sick.
how do you heal?
i can't even focus on a fucking crossword puzzle.
all i can do is stare out the window. literally.

THE WINDOW

today was the first day i didn't wake up feeling empty.
maybe this is progress? or maybe it's just because i
actually ate dinner last night. i can't tell.
is this a temporary happy? am i okay in this moment,
but only for this moment?
it comes and goes. serenity. one minute i am
completely fine, and the next my supposed wedding
song comes on at random and i have to excuse myself
to sob.
this is what time will be like: sweeping memories
taking hold of my consciousness, interrupting my
pulse.
my snapchat memories will be trash for the next year.
can't wait for those emotions to flood.
am i going to be the one he exalts out of his life, the way
i made him do to his ex?
most likely.

MARCH 8

i wish i could document this heartache accurately. it's
so hard to explain this perpetual, morbid insanity that
won't escape.
your eyes are what i see when i shut mine—
a ghost haunting me every night.
hovering over my thoughts, waiting to infiltrate at any
sign of weakness.
preying on my happiness like a sick joke.
the game of what-ifs and maybes has become my new
favorite pastime.
once the future was bright; i pictured what our family
could look like, how christmas could be ours.
now a dark fog clouds my judgement of everything
ahead.
the same image is now tear-jerking. how can i move on
when i'm stepping away from the future i once held in
my hands?
so many questions, and the only answer is that time
will tell.
something so undeniable yet so easily denied—time.
now that my time has been denied with you, i have to
ferment that time in my brain forever.

II

RUINS

INNER DRIZZLE

it is hard to picture your life
void of the reason you were living.
a future shattered, a vision destroyed
because someone couldn't love me the same.
now what do i see? what do i picture?
where i once saw a family is now empty.
reflections are reminders of loneliness,
but windows to the truth—quiet and illuminating.
reality is gloomy and overcast,
an appropriate shade of grey that begins to drizzle.
although it is raining right now,
the sun always comes out.
the sun will shine,
and so will you.

BAD SEED

toxic love is so addicting. you know it's wrong, but it
feels so right.
isn't that every mistake you've ever made?
you knew you shouldn't, but you did anyway. and shit,
it felt good.
but it was wrong and you know it.
so toxic you're shaking, and you hate it—
but you hate it even more because deep down you still
love it.
so what the fuck is wrong with you?
absolutely nothing.
toxic love is just passionate love. maybe it's not meant
to be,
but there's so much emotion behind it that it turns
moldy.
when you let something sit for too long,
it grows and eventually reveals what it's made of.
that's what toxic love is.
a bad seed you don't recognize until it sprouts and
blossoms.
but that takes time.
and eventually you see its true colors.
and by then, it's too late.
you've already planted your roots,
and it turned out ugly — but i'm in too deep now.
the only thing left is to cut it down.
cut it out of your life before the roots rot your heart
and grow so deep you feel obligated to keep watering
them.

LEARNING

it's time to learn about yourself again.
it's time to be in a relationship with you.
you once forgot what you were capable of alone,
and now you're learning it all over.
although it was nice to have some company,
sometimes they're not meant to stay forever.
it's time to do what you want to do,
and to do it for no one but yourself.

HITCHHIKER

whether you journey along this road alone for now,
it will not stay empty forever.
one day you will cross a hitchhiker—
someone you once intended to discard.

FIXER

am i a problem you wanted to fix?
you could tell all your friends how broken i was
and then you saved me.

how heroic.

UNWORTHY

why are you holding on to someone
who let you go so easily?

FIRSTS

the first heartbreak hurts.
so does the second.
and even the third.
it never gets easier, even when you think it should.
each time cuts a little deeper.

WHY

why do you put yourself through the pain and trouble
of getting your hopes up by people who have only let
you down?
if they aren't lifting you up, cut them off.
steer clear of the men who can't decide what they want,
even after you've given them everything they've asked
for.
if you have to question whether they love you,
then it's time to run.
it should never be a question.
love is not a question — it is the answer.

FALL

stop ignoring the truth,
listen to yourself.

VOYAGE

fall into the depths of my oblivion;
get lost in my pale eyes.
meander along the crevices of my body —
i'll hypnotize you with my vulnerability.
do you like how fragile i am?
how easily i break?
be careful — if you drop me, i will shatter.
explore my layers from the outside in.
some compartments are harder to crack.
dive deep into the abyss of my loneliness.
fill the void that was left on my doorstep.
if you make it through the puddle of my past,
hold on to me — it doesn't get easier.
i may be broken, but rest assured:
i've been abandoned and pieced back together before.

DEPTHS

how deep do you dare to go?
don't go if you can't handle the unknown.
crossing paths with a specimen like me can be
alluring—
for some reason, heartbreak is always enticing.

HAUNTING

to all the bad bitches out there who don't feel good
enough —
you are good enough.
and the guy making you feel any less than that
is undeserving of you.
don't date a boy who doesn't know what he wants.
date a man who sees you,
appreciates everything you've done,
and recognizes what you sacrificed for him.
rejection is a stepping stone toward accepting yourself.
your love is unique, and if he can't see that,
then he is blind to anything good.
stop feeling sorry for yourself.
feel sorry for him —
because he lost a real one.
one who would've taken care of him,
loved him unconditionally,
and would've given up anything just to earn his love.
but that version of you is gone now.
you are no longer someone who will sacrifice your
whole being
for another person.
let them sacrifice for you.
you are worthy of love,
and the one who took advantage of that
is unworthy.

III

THE ECHO

TIDE

you come in waves —
always waves of emotion,
either really good or really terrible.
sudden,
all-consuming,
and always followed
by waves of regret.
regretting the time i wasted
on someone who never deserved me,
someone who kept taking
whatever i was giving.
but i never saw it —
because i was blinded
by my love for a lost cause.
like when i was lost,
and you found me vulnerable,
picked me up, saved me.
i didn't ask for you,
but you arrived anyway,
plucked out of the universe.
and i ran like someone was chasing me —
you were chasing me.
until you caught up,
passed me,
and left me behind.
will you pick me up?
will i pick myself up?
will someone else find me?
anybody?

ENOUGH

the hardest thing about breaking up
is learning how to love yourself —
coming to terms with something
you never asked for.
instead of studying the details
of someone else,
you start learning the facets
of your own reflection.
stop projecting your insecurities
onto someone else.
put your time into what you want to do
simply because you want to do it —
and that is enough.
because before, you had to change for someone.
learn to love yourself,
because you are enough,
and no one gets to tell you otherwise,
even if they can't recognize
what makes you special.

UNSAID

don't ever stop until you find someone
that is willing to love you the same.

59

THREE WORDS

you take them for granted every single time,
because you never know when it will be the last time
you hear those three words
from the same mouth again.
what i would give to hear you say them to me again —
but like you mean it,
like how you used to mean it.
you used to love me more.
and for some reason,
it just faded away.
you never think it will be the last time
because your love feels different,
like it's built to last —
because there can't be anything in this world
that i love as much.
when did it change for you?
was there a moment you looked at me
and it didn't feel the same?
what moment made me lose you forever —
and how do i undo it?
because those three little words
are like crack to me.
what i would give to hear you say them again.
i need to feel your love,
because it once felt everlasting.

SUPERGLUE

is there a superglue
strong enough to fix
the broken heart
you left me?

MEANING

if there were a device out there
that could erase
every memory you ever made
with a person you loved,
would you use it?
would you take that pill
to forget the hurt,
the pain,
the sleepless nights
he left you with?
what is a breakup
if it isn't learning to accept
everything it carried in?
all the pain,
hurt,
hardship —
but also every lesson
that shaped you.
and what about that?
how much is a relationship worth to you?
did it break you so deeply
you'd rather erase them entirely —
the impact they had,
the way they disrupted your world?
what does it mean
to be in a meaningful relationship?

DESTROYED

you came out of the universe,
only to destroy my world
when you left.
why did you do that?

INSOMNIA

how must it feel
to be the one
who inspired an entire book?
a book
overflowing with emotion.
do you know how many nights
i spent on dates
with insomnia
just to write this?
how i had to think of you
every single fucking time
i needed to get it out of me?
i tore myself apart
over and over,
trying to find one line about you
that could capture even a fraction
of the pain you caused.
so tell me —
how must it feel?

GOOD ENOUGH

neon glow in my room —
we tossed and turned every night.
a restless bounty, everlasting.
you never gave up,
because i never slept.
nice to see you again,
insomnia.
is it what i gave
that wasn't good enough?
my all.
is it what i had
that wasn't good enough?
my heart.
is it what i asked for
that wasn't good enough?
a future.
is it what i wanted
that wasn't good enough?
forever.
is it what i told you
that wasn't good enough?
i love you.
is it what i looked like
that wasn't good enough?
a clown.
is anything i did
good enough?
because i did it all for you —
and you still let me go.

MAKEUP

how many times do i have to tell you
this isn't what i want?
if you're really doing this
for my best interest,
then do the opposite.
no breakup.
let's make up.

DEVICE

i think we hide in our phones.
our whole existence tucked inside a thin block of
technology.

REPETITION

sometimes you have to re live the pain
and make yourself feel it
over and over,
so you can remember
why you deserve so much more.

IV

THE RISE

LESSON

what heartbreak does to a girl's self-esteem
is tragic.
have you ever had your heart broken so badly
you couldn't look at yourself in the mirror?
and why is that?
when did we start believing
our reflection depends
on a man's approval.

STOP

why can't i fucking move on?
why can't i fucking sleep?
why can't i fucking hate him?
why can't i fucking love him?
they have a way of uprooting everything
without warning.
do they ever think of us?
think of how it makes us feel?
i gave you everything,
and one day you just decided
it wasn't good enough.
that's some shit.
the second they see even a hint
of possible failure,
they run —
fast,
mind made up,
never looking back.
they decide so quickly,
while i can't even decide
what to eat for dinner,
let alone make a life decision
and commit to it.
they dump everything
without a sign
and move on.
they tell their parents
faster than you ever imagined.
wow. that was quick.
i didn't realize

giving up could be that easy.
why was it so easy
to push me aside?
one minute we were cooking dinner,
the next minute
you crushed my heart.
why was it that easy
for you?
i only gave you the world,
and you crushed it —
and somehow called it
"my best interest."
but if that's true,
then why do i feel like this?
you're not just losing one person —
you're losing their family,
their friends,
their whole world.
but you don't get a warning.
you get blindsided,
broken up with,
and no chance
to say goodbye.
and it's too awkward
to reach out.
"hey... sorry your brother/sister
broke my heart.
i actually really liked you."
it's fucking sick.

BECOMING

the hardest thing about breaking up
is learning how to love yourself —
coming to terms with something
you never asked for.
instead of studying the aspects
of someone else,
you begin to love the facets
of yourself.

RISE

the hardest thing about breaking up
isn't losing them.
it's finding yourself
in the wreckage —
the pieces of you
you once gave away
like offerings,
the pieces of you
you tried to reshape
just to be loved.
but you are still here.
and you are still rising.
you survived the shattering,
the ruins,
the echo.
you learned
your own name again.
you rise —
because you always did

BECAME

i spent so long trying
to be who someone else wanted.
but somewhere between the ruin
and the rising,
i found myself again —
quiet,
certain,
whole.
i didn't become who you wanted.
i became who i needed

EPILOGUE

6 YEARS LATER

i found someone

ABOUT THE AUTHOR

Shelby Rose writes the kind of poems you read at 2 a.m. — raw, intimate, and a little too honest.

She didn't plan on publishing a book; she just needed somewhere to put the things she couldn't say out loud.

She lives in Florida.
This is her first book.